T0151050

ADIRONDACK TRAIL TIMES

With Suggested Trips From
Keene Valley, Adirondak Loj,
and Johns Brook Lodge

by Robert Denniston

completely revised and updated by
Tony Goodwin

AUSABLE PRESS
2001

Design and composition by Ausable Press.
The type is Perpetua.
Cover design by Rebecca Soderholm.

Published by Ausable Press
46 East Hill Road, Keene NY 12942

www.ausablepress.com

Library of Congress Control Number: 2001130380

ISBN 0-9672668-1-5 (pbk.; acid-free paper)

ADIRONDACK TRAIL TIMES

TABLE OF CONTENTS

FORWARD

Where shall we go today?
How long will it take us?
What is the trail like?

These and similar questions are invariably asked by a considerable number of novices and experienced climbers as they discuss their plans at breakfast, or around a campfire, and even in their homes long before they plan their trips. Then, too, there are those who, having read guide books or State literature, or climbed elsewhere, are so sure of themselves that they undertake trips far beyond their capacity. Possibly the trail information given in this little book may prove of help.

—*Robert Denniston, Keene Valley, May 1950*

INTRODUCTION

The *Guide to Adirondack Trails—High Peaks Region,* published by the Adirondack Mountain Club, describes in detail all hikes in this vicinity. *Adirondack Trail Times* is in no sense a substitute for this excellent manual, but merely a record of the writer's experiences as far as time is concerned, and a suggestion, were the hiker to spend a week in one of three places, the Adirondak Loj at Heart Lake, Johns Brook Lodge, or Keene Valley, of how these days might be well spent. Following these suggested sojourns is the writer's record of all his trail times on those paths which he has had the pleasure of hiking, or up the trailless peaks where pleasure is often mixed with some unpleasant struggling.

Knowledge of the approximate time it takes to cover mountain trails is most important if one's trip is to be successful. The times given here include those on most of the trails in the Adirondacks and the author's times in gaining the forty-six major peaks on his own particular approaches to them. This varies with many of the approaches made by others. Largely they represent times made while climbing with groups of boys whose age averaged about thirteen. Many of the trips have been taken a number of times, and the schedules tend more towards a maximum time than an average.

It is advisable to do considerable hiking and climbing over lesser peaks before attempting any of the harder or higher climbs. If a hiker is in good condition and follows these three important rules: (1) travel at a steady, slow pace, especially at the start; (2) drink but little water on the trail and do not rest for too long periods; (3) have proper footwear, there should be little difficulty in keeping up with the schedule.

In the schedule of elapsed time no mention

is made, in most cases, of either time spent on top, or in time required for descent. The latter is generally about one-third less than the time required for ascent. No trail descriptions are given but occasionally mention is made of "drinking water" conditions. All times are based on hiking without packs, unless otherwise indicated.

—R.D.

PREFACE TO THE 2001 EDITION

When Bob Denniston wrote Adirondack Trail Times over fifty years ago, he did so in part to promote hiking among the general public as a healthy and rewarding recreational pastime and to recommend the High Peaks as a desirable destination for those deciding to hike. To anyone hiking today, it should be quite apparent that he has succeeded in achieving these two goals, probably far beyond his wildest dreams. The increased numbers of hikers have resulted in many changes both here in the Adirondacks and in other mountain areas, and yet there is still much that hasn't changed. Most of the trails that the author hiked are still there, and, despite many changes in footwear and backpacks, the times reported to hike these trails remain valid. The hikes the author listed as his recommended favorites in his introductions to Keene Valley, Johns Brook Lodge, and Adirondak Loj remain the most popular in the area. Furthermore, the problem of hikers attempting trips beyond their ability remains and thus the times for specific trips in this book will continue to be a valuable resource for Adirondack hikers. Today one can also read the introductory material for its (indirect) portrayal of a slower-paced era when hikers might be expected to spend a whole week hiking from the same base and when the availability of "auto transportation" was not assumed.

While the author emphasized the ease and relative simplicity of the hiking experience in order to gain more converts, today's hikers must be sure to consult current guidebooks to become aware of the regulations in place to help protect the very resource that has attracted them in the first place. In particular, hikers must help protect the fragile alpine vegetation by only walking on bare rock or on the marked trail when above timberline.

One will also note that this guide focuses exclusively on Marcy and the High Peaks since in the author's day these were to a large extent the only part of the Adirondacks frequented by hikers. Today, by contrast, the often crowded conditions in the High Peaks have caused many hikers to seek other areas at peak use times. Included in this book are description of formerly popular trips such as the hike over Spotted Mountain to East Dix or variations of trailless climbs such as the descent from Emmons to the Rondeau's "Hermitage" on the Cold River. Although rarely done today, these descriptions have been retained with the hope that some hikers may be motivated to explore some new terrain rather than just following the "herd" up the current easiest approach to the trailless peaks.

Despite all of the changes mentioned above, the re-publication of *Adirondack Trail Times* in many ways serves to reconnect us to a previous generation and in doing that finds that the motivations and patterns of hiking in the wild have not changed one bit from fifty years ago. The original manuscript for this guide was undoubtedly pounded out on a manual typewriter and then laboriously set line by line with lead type in order for the author to share his knowledge with fellow hikers. This revision, by contrast, has been produced on a word processor and could be zapped across the country and printed in less time than it probably took for the author to drive the manuscript from Keene Valley to Elizabethtown for delivery to the printer. The author would surely marvel at how fast we can write and publish fifty years later, but I know he would be very pleased that we still hike the same trails at the same speed and that his modest effort of fifty years ago will continue to be of service to another generation of hikers.

—*Tony Goodwin, Keene, June 2001*

GENERAL NOTES & CAUTIONS

1. The guide often mentions the availability of water, but all water should now be assumed to be in need of treatment.

2. As noted in the introduction, hiking in the High Peaks is now a very popular activity compared to 1950. "The Garden" parking lot (for trips from Johns Brook Lodge) fills up late Friday or very early Saturday morning most every weekend between mid-May and Columbus Day. There is a modest daily parking charge. On weekends, a shuttle bus runs back and forth between the Garden and Marcy Field in Keene Valley to accommodate the overflow. Do not park on the road below the Garden.

3. At Adirondak Loj there is now a daily parking

fee, and this lot ususally fills up on long weekends. Currently there is no official alternate parking and no shuttle service.

4. For trips to Noonmark, the Ausable Lakes, and any other hikes on the property of the Adirondack Mountain Reserve, hikers must park at the designated parking lot just off Route 73 on the "back" or "upper" road to the Ausable Club. Dogs are not allowed in the Adirondack Mountain Preserve.

5. Reservations for Adirondak Loj and Johns Brook Lodge may be made by mail at P.O. Box 867, Lake Placid, NY 12946 or by phone at 518-523-3441.

6. Hikers must help protect the fragile alpine vegetation by only walking on bare rock or on the marked trail when above timberline.

7. Always carry water, flashlight, matches, rain gear, map, and warm clothing (not cotton). Weather changes can be dramatic and sudden, even in summer.

Suggested Trips from
ADIRONDAK LOJ

Heart Lake, eight miles from Lake Placid, is the property of the Adirondack Mountain Club (ADK). The ADK operates Adirondak Loj (Melville Dewey's "simplified spelling" from the days when the Loj was owned by the Lake Placid Club) which provides meals and lodging plus cabins, lean-tos, and campsites for rent at a nominal fee.

Upon arriving at Adirondak Loj, and providing you still have around two hours before the supper bell rings, a trip up Mt. Jo is suggested. There are two routes, a short steep ascent which can easily be done in half an hour, and a longer route that takes about fifty minutes.

For your second day, consider a trip into Indian Pass with lunch at the Summit Rock, where you may look up at the cliffs of Wallface and down toward the Santanoni country. On the way back, if you feel energetic, a walk up the trail to Scott's Pond is rewarding, and either going or coming be sure and make a detour down to Rocky Falls lean-to where you may be tempted to take a plunge in the brook.

The MacIntyre Range should next receive your attention. This is one of the better climbs in the mountains. There are four peaks in this range: Wright, Algonquin, Iroquois, and Marshall. The last named should not be tried on the same day as the others as the bushwacking between it and Iroquois is very rough and the distance is much farther than it appears. Wright may be done alone, Algonquin alone, or Wright done on the way up before climbing Algonquin. Adding Iroquois makes it a tough day, but if you are up to it you can vary the trip by coming back through Avalanche Pass as you take the trail down to Colden Lake instead of reclimbing the dome of Algonquin. However, going through Avalanche Pass will add considerable mileage to your day's outing.

Phelps is a relatively easy climb with a superb view of Marcy from its summit ledge. Climbing this mountain would be a good day's venture after doing Algonquin.

Colden is one of the most attractive and yet steepest mountains to climb and might well be your fifth day's adventure. The usual route is to walk in to Colden Lake, climb it from there, and return via Lake Arnold. Some prefer to do this trip in reverse. Ascending Colden by the Trap Dyke is a sporty climb that should not be taken unless you are a good climber and have preferably talked to someone who has done it. Several hikers have got into trouble on this particular climb; yet it is not dangerous if caution is taken. There is no trail and the climb up the dyke begins at Avalanche Lake, across from the "Hitch-up-Matilda" bridge. The danger of the trip is coming out on the slide too soon.

For your final day Marcy is listed. This mountain, via the Van Hoevenberg trail, is an interesting climb, and it has the beautiful Indian Falls about half-way up. When climbing from the Loj the writer likes to climb up via Lake Arnold and Lake Tear of the Clouds, with an hour's detour to do Skylight, and then come back by the Van Hoevenberg trail. However, this is a much longer and more rigorous trip.

Granted additional time, with Adirondack Loj as a base, you can also climb on different days Whiteface and Esther; Cascade and Porter (a short day's trip); Pitchoff (not a 4,000 foot peak but one of the most interesting climbs in the Adirondacks); Street and Nye (a bushwack of the two least pleasant of the 4,000 foot peaks); Tabletop (another bushwack with not much of a view but the chance of lunch and a good rest at Indian Falls after you have climbed it); Gray Peak (it can be done on the day you do Marcy via Lake Arnold in place of Skylight); and Marshall (another very long day's trip from the Loj). You will need auto transportation to do Esther, Whiteface, Cascade, Porter, and Pitchoff.

Suggested Trips from
KEENE VALLEY

Keene Valley is a mecca for mountain climbers. Here, it is possible not only to climb the tallest of the Adirondack peaks, but also to make numerous day trips on lesser peaks all of which give magnificent views of the surrounding mountains and valley.

The number of possible trips from Keene Valley is so great that it is difficult to know where to start. As a likely warm-up trip for the first day, Noonmark is suggested. The trail, starting from the golf course of the Ausable Club at St. Hubert's, is not a long one, and although steep in parts, is well maintained and well worth a leisurely first day. It can be done in a morning or an afternoon, but it would be far better to spend the whole day on it.

Looking towards the east from the summit of Noonmark stands Giant, the favorite mountain for most residents of Keene Valley, and this would be an ideal peak to climb next. The trail is magnificently kept up by the Adirondack Trail Improvement Society; it is long, steep in certain sections, but not too difficult. The last sure water on the trail is found when you cross Roaring Brook. Incidently, be sure and take a few minutes detour to see the lookout above Roaring Brook Falls. A whole day is needed for Giant to get its full benefit. If you feel particularly energetic and can spare another two hours and a half, the trip to Rocky Ridge Peak (Giant's Wife) will give you some good ledge climbing.

If your visit to the Adirondacks does not include a stay at Johns Brook Lodge, the third day could well be spent in walking into the Lodge and possibly climbing Big Slide or Short Job before returning to the Garden at the head of Interbrook Road where you have left your car.

It would be well to take it easy your fourth day by climbing one of the following: Baxter, Spread Eagle, Owl's Head, or Hurricane. The first two can be climbed directly from Keene Valley, while, to reach the others, a short drive is necessary.

The Ausable Lakes are beauty spots in the Adirondacks. They are privately owned but hikers are welcome. A good trip would be to climb Colvin, diverging from the Lake Road at 2 miles and ascending via the Gill Brook Trail. On the return, turn left and take in Fish Hawk Cliffs and Indian Head on the descent to the Lake Road just above the boathouse. Those who still have some ambition may return via the East or West River Trails which are very scenic and only marginally longer than walking the Lake Road.

Dix is one of the better Adirondack peaks and well merits your consideration for the final day of your week's stay. This trail starts at the same spot where you park your car when climbing Noonmark, but is a much longer expedition, and requires a full day. The trail is steep and apt to be wet. Be sure and visit the Beckhorn, the southern tip of Dix to which a trail leads you in a few minutes. You may have an inclination to drop down into Hunter's Pass, but it is a good two hour round trip, and requires a one thousand foot ascent to get back to the trail.

No mention has been made of Twin, Snow, Rooster Comb, Tripod, Hopkins, the Cascade-Porter circuit, Round Mountain, and other peaks which vary in time and energy consuming qualities. Then, too, Keene Valley abounds in wonderful woods walks, not to mention other peaks which can be reached by a half hour or so drive.

Suggested Trips From
JOHNS BROOK LODGE

By spending a week at the Johns Brook Lodge, three and a half miles from the "Garden" in Keene Valley, it is possible to do pretty thoroughly all the peaks in this area.

The Lodge, owned and operated by the Adirondack Mountain Club, makes an ideal base. It is open to the public.

Assuming that you arrive at Johns Brook Lodge in the early afternoon, a jaunt up Short Job before supper is suggested, followed perhaps by a plunge in the stream.

For your first full day of mountain climbing the Big Slide circuit makes a good starter. The best way to climb Big Slide is to follow for half the trip the brook that bears its name. The view from Big Slide is particularly impressive. In returning continue on over Yard and down into Klondike

Notch (sometimes erroneously known as Railroad Notch). The return trip is about twice as long but easy and you should be back at Johns Brook Lodge in the middle of the afternoon.

Marcy, because it is the highest mountain in the State, is a peak usually sought after. It is a long haul, requiring an early start. The best method of approach is to go up by the Hopkins trail and return via Slant Rock, although since your later trips may twice take you over part of the Slant Rock trail, you might prefer to return also by the Hopkins trail. This is generally wet at all times of the year, especially as you near the Van Hoevenberg trail. Incidentally, the last water is at the former site of the Plateau Lean-to, .4 miles from the junction with the Van Hoevenberg Trail.

Gothics, by the way of the Orebed Brook Trail, is a wonderful climb, and just the expedition for your fourth day. After reaching the summit you may return over Armstrong and Upper Wolf Jaws. Some prefer to do this part of the Range in reverse so that the highest of the peaks of the day will be climbed last, but I have found it easier to do Gothics first. Armstrong has a good lookout, but Upper Wolf Jaws offers but little in the way of a view. Upon reaching the notch between the two Wolf Jaws, you can decide whether you wish to take an extra hour to do Lower Wolf Jaws. There is no water on this trip after you leave Gothics Lean-to until you reach a brook well down the trail towards the Lodge from the Wolf Jaws Notch.

Haystack is the writer's favorite peak but to be really appreciated it should be done on a good day. The best approach is from Bushnell Falls to Slant Rock and then up that trail to where it joins the Range Trail. Then comes that very steep bit of climbing known as the Devil's Half Mile, before you leave the Range trail for the pull over Little Haystack and on up to the top of Haystack. The same route of return is suggested although it is possible to combine it with Basin and Saddleback.

For your final day's trip, start off the same way as you had in climbing Haystack but at the Slant Rock Lean-to cross the stream and take the steep but beautiful cut-off which lands you a few hundred yards east of the former site of the Snobird Lean-to on the Range Trail. You should reach the top of Basin about lunch time, and after admiring the beautiful views that this peak offers, scramble down off it and up steep Saddleback. Then on down to the col between that mountain and Gothics and back to the Lodge via the Orebed Brook Trail.

Granted that you have been in good hiking condition and have had favorable weather, you will have in a week's time climbed nine of the four thousand foot peaks plus several lesser summits. Should you feel inclined to take it easy durning your stay at Johns Brook Lodge there is no more restful place to sit and take in the beauty of the mountains than the porch of this mountain retreat.

MARCY AND APPROACHES

JOHNS BROOK LODGE
From Keene Valley, with Packs

Leave the Garden	0
Deer Brook	:40
Ranger's Cabin	1:30
Johns Brook Lodge	1:40

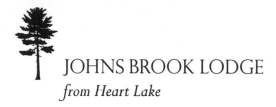

JOHNS BROOK LODGE
from Heart Lake

Leave parking area at end of South Meadows Road	0
Klondike Lean-to	:00
Top of Klondike Notch	1:30
Big Slide Trail Junction	1:40
Johns Brook Lodge	2:15

MARCY

From Johns Brook Lodge via Hopkins Trail

Leave Johns Brook Lodge	0
Hogback Brook	:25
Bushnell Falls Trail Junction	:45
Van Hoevenberg Trail	2:35
Plateau Lean-to site (last water)	2:45
Summit of Marcy	3:25

MARCY

From Johns Brook Lodge via Slant Rock Trail

Leave Johns Brook Lodge	0
Hogback Brook	:25
Bushnell Falls Trail Junction	:45
Slant Rock	1:45
Range Trail	2:35
Summit of Marcy	3:55

MARCY

From Heart Lake via Van Hoevenberg Trail

Leave Adirondak Loj	0
Marcy Dam	:50
Indian Falls	1:55
Hopkins Trail Junction	2:55
Plateau Lean-to Site	3:05
Summit of Marcy	3:45

MARCY
From Heart Lake via Lake Arnold

Leave Adirondak Loj	0
Marcy Dam	:50
Avalanche Lean-to	1:15
Arrive Lake Arnold and trail junction to Mt. Colden	2:15
Leave Lake Arnold	2:25
Feldspar Lean-to	3:05
Lake Tear of the Clouds (last water)	4:05
Four Corners	4:15
Summit of Marcy	5:00

MARCY
From Colden Lake via Opalescent Stream

Leave Colden Dam	0
Opalescent Flume	:35
Uphill Lean-to	1:15
Feldspar Lean-to	1:30
Lake Tear of the Clouds (last water)	2:30
Four Corners	2:40
Summit of Marcy	3:25

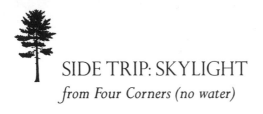

SIDE TRIP: SKYLIGHT
from Four Corners (no water)

leave Four Corners	0
Summit of Skylight	:30

SIDE TRIP: GRAY PEAK

From Lake Tear (trailless, no water)

Leave Trail at outlet of Lake Tear	0
Summit of Gray Peak	:35

SIDE TRIP: CLIFF

From Uphill Lean-to (trailless, no water)

Leave Uphill Lean-to	0
Junction with abandoned Twin Brook Trail	:03
Junction with herd path at height of land	:15
Summit of Cliff	1:10

SIDE TRIP: REDFIELD
From Uphill Lean-to (trailless)

Leave Uphill Lean-to	0
Top of falls on tributary Uphill Brook	:50
Leave brook (last water)	1:05
Summit of Redfield	2:05

SIDE TRIP: TABLETOP
From Indian Falls (trailless, no water)

Leave Indian Falls	0
Summit of Tabletop	1:05

SIDE TRIP: PHELPS

From Above Marcy Dam (no water)

Leave junction one mile above Marcy Dam	0
Summit of Phelps	1:50

THE RANGE TRAIL

UPPER WOLF JAWS, ARMSTRONG, & GOTHICS

Heading West from Johns Brook Lodge

Leave Johns Brook Lodge	0
Wolf Jaws Lean-to (last water twenty minutes above lean-to)	:35
Wolf Jaws Notch	1:15
Summit of Upper Wolf Jaws	2:25
Summit of Armstrong (suggest lunch here)	3:15
Summit of Gothics	3:50
West peak of Gothics	4:05
Gothics Col	4:25
Johns Brook Lodge via Orebed Trail	6:00

SIDE TRIP: LOWER WOLF JAWS

From White Trail / Range Trail Junction
(no water)

Leave White Trail / Range Trail Junction in Notch	0
Junction of Wedge Brook Trail	:12
Summit Lower Wolf Jaws	:35

BASIN, SADDLEBACK, GOTHICS, & ARMSTRONG

Heading East from Johns Brook Lodge

Leave Johns Brook Lodge	0
Hogback Brook	:25
Bushnell Falls Trail Junction	:45
Slant Rock	1:45
Junction with Shorey Shortcut (last water)	2:00
Range Trail via Shorey Shortcut	2:50
Summit of Basin	3:45
Leave Summit of Basin (after lunch)	4:45
Summit of Saddleback	5:40
Leave Summit of Saddleback	5:55
Gothics Col	6:15
(Returning to Lodge from here via Orebed Trail would take one hour and thirty-five minutes)	
West peak of Gothics	6:45

Summit of Gothics	7:00
Leave Summit of Gothics	7:15
Summit of Armstrong	7:45
Summit of Upper Wolf Jaws	8:25
Wolf Jaws Notch	9:00
Wolf Jaws Lean-to	9:30
Johns Brook Lodge (via cutoff)	10:00

HAYSTACK

From Johns Brook Lodge

Leave Johns Brook Lodge	0
Hogback Brook	:25
Bushnell Falls Trail Junction	:45
Slant Rock	1:45
Junction with Shorey Shortcut	1:50
Range Trail/Slant Rock Trail Junction	2:30
Range Trail/Haystack Trail Junction	3:05
Summit of Little Haystack	3:15
Summit of Haystack	3:40

HAYSTACK, BASIN, & SADDLEBACK
From Johns Brook Lodge

Leave Johns Brook Lodge	0
Summit of Haystack (as described on page 37)	3:40
Range Trail / Haystack Trail Junction	4:05
Former Snobird Lean-to site	4:30
Leave Snobird Lean-to site	4:45
Junction with Shorey Shortcut	4:55
Summit of Basin	5:40
Leave Summit of Basin	5:55
Summit of Saddleback	6:50
Gothics Col	7:10
Johns Brook Lodge	8:45

HAYSTACK

When doing Marcy via Slant Rock (no water)

Allow two hours (exclusive of stay on top of Haystack) from Slant Rock Trail Junction and return. Returning via former Snobird Lean-to site and Shorey Shortcut takes an extra forty-five minutes.

GOTHICS
Via Orebed Brook Trail

Leave Johns Brook Lodge	0
Gothics Col	1:55
West Peak of Gothics	2:25
Summit of Gothics	2:40

BIG SLIDE
Return via Yard

Leave Johns Brook Lodge	0
Leave Big Slide Brook	1:00
Summit of Big Slide	2:15
Leave Summit of Big Slide	3:15
Klondike Trail Junction	5:00
Johns Brook Lodge	5:35

SHORT JOB
From Johns Brook Lodge

Leave Johns Brook Lodge	0
Summit of Short Job	:30

THE MACINTYRE RANGE

ALGONQUIN

From Heart Lake

Leave Adirondak Loj	0
Junction of Algonquin Trail	:25
Falls (last sure water)	1:30
Wright Trail Junction	1:50
Summit of Algonquin	2:45

ALGONQUIN

From Lake Colden

Leave Ranger's Cabin at Colden Lake	0
Start MacIntyre Trail	:05
Iroquois Trail Junction (cairn of stones)	1:30
Plateau	1:33
Summit of Algonquin	1:55

IROQUOIS
From Lake Colden / Algonquin Trail
(poor trail, no water)

Leave cairn of stones	0
Top of Boundary Peak	:15
Summit of Iroquois	:40

WRIGHT

From Heart Lake (no water)

Leave Adirondak Loj	0
Leave Algonquin Trail	1:50
Summit of Wright	2:15

MARSHALL
From Flowed Lands (trailless)

Leave Flowed Lands, following Herbert Brook	0
Notch (leave brook, last water)	1:35
Summit of Marshall	2:00
Lookout, north end of ridge	2:20

COLDEN

COLDEN
From Adirondak Loj via Lake Colden

Leave Adirondak Loj	0
Marcy Dam	:50
Avalanche Lean-to	1:15
Head of Avalanche Pass	1:40
Junction with trail around northwest shore of Lake Colden	2:20
Start of Colden Trail (east side of lake)	2:45
Summit of Colden	4:20

COLDEN

From Adirondak Loj via Trap Dyke

Leave Adirondak Loj	0
Marcy Dam	:50
Avalanche Lean-to	1:15
Head of Avalanche Pass	1:30
Leave trail at outlet of Avalanche Pass	1:50
Start of dyke	1:55
Out on face of slide	3:00
Summit of Colden	3:45

COLDEN
From Adirondak Loj via Lake Arnold

Leave Adirondak Loj	0
Marcy Dam	:50
Avalanche Lean-to	1:15
Trail junction to Colden at Lake Arnold	2:15
Summit of Colden	3:15

WHITEFACE & ESTHER

Times on climbing Whiteface were made on the old Wilmington Trail which was rerouted and made considerably longer due to (1940's) ski developments on Marble Mountain (now abandoned in favor of the present Whiteface Ski Area which opened in 1958). The best way of approach from the Wilmington area is now up from the Atmospheric Sciences Research Center following the abandoned lift line. It will probably take two and one half hours. Herd path to Esther diverges right one mile from the summit of Marble Mountain. Time to reach Esther from the Wilmington trail is about forty-five minutes.

KEENE VALLEY & ST. HUBERT'S

BAXTER

from Upham Cottage, Beede Road, Keene Valley

Leave Beede Road	0
Start Baxter Trail	:04
West Peak	:55
Summit of Baxter	1:05
East Peak	1:15
Edge of Beede Farm	1:50
Beede Road at farmhouse	1:55
Road for Upham Cottage	2:07

GIANT

Via Roaring Brook Trail, St. Hubert's

Leave Route 73 opposite south road to Ausable Club	0
Junction of trail to head of Roaring Brook Falls	:15
Cross Roaring Brook (last water)	:40
Open ledge and lookout	1:25
Leave open ledge and lookout	1:40
Junction of Zander Scott (Ridge) Trail	2:05
False summit of Giant	2:15
Summit of Giant	2:40

SIDE TRIP: ROCKY RIDGE PEAK (GIANT'S WIFE)

From Summit of Giant

Leave summit of Giant	0
Leave Roaring Brook Trail to descend ledges	:05
Bottom of col between peaks	:35
Summit of Rocky Ridge Peak	1:05

Allow about ten minutes more for return trip.

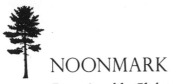

NOONMARK

From Ausable Club Golf Course, St. Hubert's

Leave Golf Course	0
Leave Dix Trail	:25
Summit of Noonmark	1:50

DIX

*From Ausable Club Golf Course, St. Hubert's
(with packs)*

Leave Golf Course	0
Round Pond trail junction	1:25
Boquet River Lean-to (without packs)	2:45
Base of slide (last water)	3:30
Hunter's Pass trail junction	4:30
Summit of Dix	5:00

HUNTER'S PASS

From St. Hubert's / Dix Trail (very steep)

Start from Dix/Hunter's Pass trail junction	0
Hunter's Pass	:45
Arrive back at Dix/Hunter's Pass trail junction	1:45

HOUGH
From Summit of Dix

A relatively good herd path. The time for a round trip from the Summit of Dix to the summit of Hough and back is two and one-half hours.

SAWTEETH

*Via Scenic Trail from Lower Ausable Lake
(rough and very steep)*

Leave Lower Ausable Lake	0
First ledges, view of Lower Lake	:35
Main ledges, view of Lower Lake	:47
Next outlook	1:30
Summit of Sawteeth	2:55

DIAL & NIPPLETOP
From Boquet River Lean-to, St. Hubert's
(no water, part trailless)

Leave Boquet River Lean-to	0
Summit of Dial after bushwacking	1:30
Summit of Nippletop via trail from Dial	2:45

COLVIN

From St. Hubert's

Leave Ausable Club "Gate"	0
Start of Colvin Trail on Ausable Lake Road	:50
Gill Brook Trail junction	1:05
Indian Head Trail junction	1:10
Elk Pass Trail juntion	1:50
Summit of Colvin	2:40

BLAKE'S PEAK

From Summit of Colvin (no water, steep)

Leave summit of Colvin	0
Upper Ausable Lake Trail junction in notch	:25
Summit of Blake's Peak	:50

Allow a good hour for return trip.

ELK PASS & NIPPLETOP
From Colvin Trail / Elk Pass Trail Junction

Leave Colvin Trail / Elk Pass Trail junction	0
Elk Pass	:35
Summit of Nippletop	1:45

ROOSTER COMB
From Route 73, Keene Valley (no water)

Leave parking area on Route 73 just south of Keene Valley	0
School Pond	:05
Junction connector to Sachs Trail	:25
Sachs Trail / Hedgehog Trail Junction	1:10
Junction of side trail to view	1:20
Summit of Rooster Comb	1:40

TWIN (THE BROTHERS)
& BIG SLIDE

From Keene Valley (no water)

Leave the Garden	0
First ledges	:35
Top of first peak	1:10
Top of second peak	1:25
Top of third Brother	2:10
Stream (last water)	2:40
Junction of Slide Mountain Brook Trail	3:00
Summit of Big Slide	3:15

SPREAD EAGLE
From Keene Valley (no water)

Acccss from Phelps Brook Road as described in the original edition is currently difficult due to a trail closure by a private landowner. For those who can find their way from Beede Road via the private road system, however, the trail is maintained to the summit of Spread Eagle and on to the summit of Hopkins in about another thirty minutes.

Leave car at end of Beede Road	0
Hopkins Trail junction (top of road system)	:50
First lookout	1:15
Surveyor's Top	1:30
Summit of Spread Eagle	1:35

HEART LAKE

STREET & NYE
From Adirondak Loj (trailless)

Leave Adirondak Loj	0
Junction of old Nye Ski Trail	:15
Indian Pass Brook (last water)	:45
Summit of Street	3:45
Leave Summit of Street (after lunch)	4:45
Summit of Nye	6:00

A herd path has recently been established and very minimally marked. Navigational skill is still required to follow this route, and an admonition that was in the original edition still applies: do *not* go too far north or follow lumber trails.

JO
From Adirondak Loj

Leave Adirondak Loj	0
Summit of Jo (by short route)	:30
Summit of Jo (by long route)	:50

VAN HOEVENBERG

From South Meadow Road (no water)

Leave South Meadow Road at trail entrance   :0
Summit of Van Hoevenberg   1:00

Fifteen minutes beyond the summit is the top of the old bobsled run and the new bob/luge combined track. Hikers have traditionally been able to walk down along the run and out through the gate without charge.

INDIAN PASS & SUMMIT ROCK
From Adirondak Loj

Leave Adirondak Loj	0
Rocky Falls Trail Junction	:50
Scott's Clearing (broken dam)	1:40
Leave stream to Scott's Pond	2:05
Top of Pass	2:40
Summit Rock	3:00

This trail continues on to the old mining camp at Tahawus, but it is too long for a single day's round trip. However, if you leave a car at the far end before you begin, it can be done in about seven hours.

THE DIX RANGE

SPOTTED, EAST DIX, SOUTH DIX, & MACOMB
From Route 73

Leave Route 73 (100 yards north of the junction with Route 9	:0
End of woods trail. Cross from south side	:45
Cross main fork of South Branch	1:10
Summit of Spotted Mountain	3:10
Summit of East Dix	4:20
Summit of South Dix	5:30
Summit of Macomb	6:30
Elk Lake/Dix Trail	8:35
Elk Lake Road	9:15

Note that no time is allowed for stops on mountain tops, nor for lunch.

Although this trip as described is still doable in about the same time, the currently preferred route to East Dix starts on the North Fork of the Boquet (one and one-half miles north of the junction with Route 9) and ascends via the slide rather than over Spotted Mountain, which is now considerably more grown up in the aftermath of the 1908 fire.

THE SANTANONI COUNTRY

DUCK HOLE

*From Tupper Lake Highway Ten Miles from
Saranac Lake (with packs)*

Leave parking place on fire road that goes by Corey's and Axton Lean-to	0
Trail crosses another fire road	:35
Blueberry Pond (on left)	1:05
Clearing and Duck Hole Fire Road	2:05
Arrive Ward Brook Lean-to	2:20
Leave Ward Brook Lean-to	2:50
Number 4 Lean-to's	3:08
Meadows	4:00
Northville-Lake Placid Trail junction	4:20
Cold River Lean-to's	4:30
Duck Hole	5:05

SANTANONI, PANTHER PEAK, & COUCHSACHRAGA

From Duck Hole (mostly trailless)

Very few hikers currently descend from Couch-sachraga to the Northville-Lake Placid Trail as described below. All three summits, however, are now reached by good herd paths which leave the marked trail at a beaver dam three-tenths of a mile south of Santanoni Lean-to. With these herd paths, the times as far as the summit of Couchsa-chraga should be about one-third less. The descent from Couchsachraga and return to the Duck Hole should be about the same.

Leave Duck Hole	0
Lumber clearing	:50
Start of herd path	1:50
Trail to Santanoni	2:02
Summit of Santanoni	4:00

Leave summit of Santanoni (after lunch)	4:30
Summit of Panther Peak	6:15
Leave Summit of Panther Peak	6:45
Summit of Couchsachraga	9:15
Leave summit of Couchsachraga	9:30
Northville-Lake Placid Trail (Hermit's)	12:15
Duck Hole	14:15

SEYMOUR

From Ward Brook Lean-to (trailless)

Leave Ward Brook Lean-to   0
Summit of Seymour   1:50

SEWARD, DONALDSON, & EMMONS

From Ward Brook Lean-to

(trailless, no water on peaks)

There are now established herd paths as far as Emmons, and most hikers currently return from Emmons along the ridge to Ward Brook. The trip as described below, however, makes for a longer but more interesting tour of this remote country.

Leave Ward Brook Lean-to	0
Summit of Seward	3:55
Leave summit of Seward (after lunch)	4:25
Summit of Donaldson	5:55
Leave summit of Donaldson	6:05
Summit of Emmons	7:10
Leave summit of Emmons to go down to Cold River	7:25
Northville-Lake Placid Trail	9:35

West Gate of Rondeau's City of Cold River	9:43
Leave Hermit's	10:00
Ward Brook Lean-to	12:15

MISCELLANEOUS

CASCADE

From Cascade Lakes Road (Route 73)

Leave Cascade Lakes Road (above lakes)   0
Cascade/Porter Trail junction   1:40
Summit of Cascade   1:50

PORTER
From Cascade / Porter Trail Junction

Leave Cascade/Porter junction	0
Summit of Porter	:30

PITCHOFF

From Cascade Lakes Road (Route 86) (no water)

Leave highway opposite Cascade Trail start	0
First lookout over Cascade Lakes	:30
Traverse below the cliffs	1:00
Junction with side trail to ledge	
& boulders	1:15
Summit of Pitchoff	2:10
Top of last peak of range	3:20
Arrive highway (2.5 miles down road	
from start)	4:00

HURRICANE
From Parking Area at End of Dirt Road
from Elizabethtown

Leave car	0
Site of Observer's Cabin	:50
Summit of Hurricane	1:15

ROUND MOUNTAIN
From St. Hubert's Dix Trail (no water)

Leave St. Hubert's Dix Trail at top of Notch   0
Summit of Round Mountain   1:15

AMPERSAND

From Saranac Lake / Tupper Lake Highway

Leave highway	0
Arrive at site of former observer's cabin (last water)	:45
Summit of Ampersand	1:40

POK-O-MOONSHINE
From Route 9 South of Keeseville

Leave Route 9	0
Cave	:15
Top of first cliffs	:20
Lean-to at site of former observer's cabin	:45
Summit of Pok-o-Moonshine	
by short steep route	:55
by longer more gradual route	1:00

CHIEF'S PEAK
(CARL MOUNTAIN)
From Summit of Pok-o-Moonshine (trailless)

Leave Summit of Pok-o-Moonshine	0
Summit of Chief's Peak	1:05

Caution: while this peak does offer a unique and seldom-visited summit and view, damage caused by the January 1998 ice storm has likely as much as doubled the time required to reach the summit.

INDEX OF TRAIL TIMES

Ausable Press publishes books about the Adirondacks under the name Bark Eater Books. The local Algonquin called their Iroquois enemies *adirondacks*, or bark-eaters, implying that they were such poor hunters that they, like the deer, would be reduced to eating bark in the winters. Since books are also bark-eaters, it seems a fitting name.

This is a Bark Eater book.